Skipper

Acknowledgements

With thanks to the editors of the following, where some of these poems first appeared: *Envoi, The Journal, Magma, The North, The Reader*, and *The Wolf.* A number of poems were first published as the pamphlet, *Armour* (smith|doorstop, 2011). Sections of 'Grace Darling's ABC' were included in *Oxford Poets 2013* (Carcanet, 2013). 'Saint Cuthbert Banishes Demons from the Laser Clinic' first appeared in the pamphlet, *Shadowscript* (University of Newcastle, 2013). 'Waiting for the Wounded' was commissioned for the 'Screaming Steel' exhibition at Hatton Gallery, Newcastle-upon-Tyne, 2014. 'Knots', '8th Wonder', 'Horse's Mouth', 'Tradition', 'Trolleyology' and 'Harbour Master' were first published in *Tyne View* (New Writing North, 2012).

Thanks also to: Linda Anderson, Birtley Aris, Paul Batchelor, Charles Bell, Michael Chaplin, Linda France, Cynthia Fuller, Bill Herbert, Naomi Jaffa and all at the Aldeburgh 8 Seminar, Jenny Larby, Pippa Little, Claire Malcolm, Lisa Matthews, Sean O'Brien, Ellen Phethean, Anne Ryland, Bruce Woodcock, and Anna Woodford.

'Meet the Victorians' draws on the research of Matthew Sweet, and his book *Inventing the Victorians*.

Skipper
Christy Ducker

smith|doorstop

Published 2015 by
smith|doorstop Books
The Poetry Business
Bank Street Arts
32-40 Bank Street
Sheffield S1 2DS
www.poetrybusiness.co.uk

ISBN 978-1-910367-36-0

British Library Cataloguing-in-Publication Data.
A catalogue record for this book is available from the
British Library.

Typeset by Utter
Printed by Printondemand.com
Cover image: iStockphoto.com

smith|doorstop is a member of Inpress,
www.inpressbooks.co.uk. Distributed by Central Books Ltd.,
99 Wallis Road, London E9 5LN.

The Poetry Business is an Arts Council
National Portfolio Organisation

Supported by
**ARTS COUNCIL
ENGLAND**

Contents

for my family

And

suddenly you are here
and I am astonished
by the way you smell of bloody bread
and the way you already decide
to place a webbed hand here,
to slow-wink a newt's eye there.
I am astonished that you are purple.

And now I know glee
at the indignant heaving bellows of your belly,
your self-startled arms flung wide proclaiming
your tiny chimp gums.

And I watch to see time
measured by your face,
crane as you push each new word through glottal air.
I thrill because you're not like me
but you and young and other.

Skeletons

At what point do we say *There. It stops there*
and decide to forgive the man whose family
once shipped slaves, or the woman whose father
upset a nation with rumours and guns?

Perhaps it's the point at which I would say
my husband's family used to duck witches
but when I nearly drown, off Galway Bay
one night, he swims for me and helps me breathe.

Perhaps it's the point at which I would say
yes it's a beautiful ivory box
of the heirloom his mother displays
detached from the blood of its carving out.

Perhaps it's the point at which I might learn
to love the present flesh that softens bone.

[handwritten margin notes, left:] Don't love this / not your / place to / say this / not your place / to forgive

[handwritten margin notes, right:] also witch trials / were a / symptom of / mysogeny + / often xenephobi / are still experienca / mysogeny today / so I'm not / over it even / if you / are.

Getting Rid of the Aphids

Instead of a way out
she finds a sack.

It arrives at the greenhouse
each Thursday.

Once set down,
the sack fidgets

until she loosens it
and pours out

one kilo of ladybirds.

For a moment
she sees only

stunned treasure
hissing to a standstill

but soon
the ladybirds fly
whirring.

Hunting, they stud
the soft hurt
of tomato stems.

At night
they fall from her clothes –
brilliant

even in darkness.

At The Hepworth

I try not to panic, when she tells me
about my *strong aura*, how pink it is
against the gallery wall in the sun,
that I walk with spirits, *one tall, one busty*.

This couldn't happen where I come from
because she'd be mad, and I would run
like anyone born at England's edge
where the dead drown and we leave them

but this is Wakefield, built inland on barley.
The woman is sane in the same way
a good librarian is sane, with a sheer
commitment to fact. I have to ask

if they're always here, Busty and Lanky,
when they might leave and whether I've trod
on their toes, or if I should feed them.
She says they're happy and here beside me

in Gallery 6, where objects insist
we hold them, though we cannot,
and my favourite is 'Landscape Sculpture'
because it shows the strings that connect us.

Saint Cuthbert Banishes Demons from the Laser Clinic

He's sad to see my tattoo go
under the laser, blistering
from Lindisfarne knot to hot dough,
I got inked-up too young –
too full of hell, I say to him
and he smiles his hermit crab smile,
suggests I think of the Book
his acolyte wrote on skin
with soot and gold, how it reconciles
gannets, cats and dogs as word
of love, how every page is flawed
on purpose, saying to people
perfection makes us much too proud –
wear your mistakes like gospel.

The Working Woman's Right Breast is Not Amused

Yes, I tried to be patient and fair
when she told me about her career,
forgetting that I can express myself too
in the strongest of possible terms.

But Number One child, she rushed him away
so he barely remembers my name
and Number Two is already dispatched
down to *Kidz in a Tizz with Nadine*.

So I thought I might spook her a bit
with a hint at some salt in my works,
which is why I lie here teat up
for inspection in hospital greens.

As we stare at my gubbins on screen,
my nodes come up pouting like mouths
that are movie star blooming and clear –
she concedes that she must be *run down*

so with luck, a bit later, she'll take me
out rowing and dabble a hand
down my stoup, while I ask for more kids
who I secretly hope will be hungry, and male (and twins).

Knots

– The Volunteer Life Brigade Museum, South Shields

In two glass cases, three hundred answers
to all the questions of disconnection
we've had so far. The man overboard,
the stray boat, the matter of where to hang
one's hammock – these we resolve with a *clew*
a *strop*, or the ever-loyal *what knot*
and if loose ends remain a problem,
the *splice* or *surgeon* will bring them in line –

so when we want to hold on to something
that seems hard to grasp, the future let's say,
it pays to listen to Tom, an old hand
who readies lifelines in the watch-house shed
before he points out the thing we're best at
is *rescue and all its inventions.*

Entering the Country

The soles of your feet haven't touched the ground
but still you're asked to *wait in line* with all

the wall-eyed grown-ups. I hold you aloft
so you can see how other babies globe

their cheeks at you, as you begin to breach
the hush that cramps us in this hall. You light

on children's sounds, until you've hawked
your English *da da da* for Xhosan clicks

that dovetail with Punjabi *bah* then pitch
into Malayan *neeyangs* before a flit

towards the ceiling. Airline staff worry
our papers. New flights arrive and depart.

Small wonder then, that two days on
as we cut bread and lay out plates you stun

us all when down the runway of your tongue
your first word comes. *Aeroplane.* Its wings

fuelled by a lifetime, it circles our lunch
three times, then zooms out the door through a cloud

of mosquitoes. We watch it recede,
feeling the tremor of journeys begun.

8th Wonder

If I ever get to the Taj Mahal,
or land on the moon, or phone my sister
right from the top of Burj Khalifa,
I know I'll feel like I do down here, cheating

nature, breathing tightly, wondering how
the human hand can be so slight
yet bring about marvels. Eighty-five feet
below high water, anything's possible

even a walk from shore to shore in air
that's engineered to be here. This tunnel
hums with neon light against the awful
press of soil, the trillion weight of Tyne

moving so close I think I might hear
the tides heave, the silt creep, a faint tectonics
grumbling away below the echoic
manoeuvres of ships which skim past my head

while the escalators pomp out a tune
to mark the tunnel's sixtieth birthday
under the river, its sunken beauty
party to few but the seals' ovations.

Descent

It was my kick that did it, made you shout
Hooligan! made me clatter the beer can
along the Quayside and into the past –
to Hoolihan, great great grandad Molloy

who bowls at me on the wheels of his name
allowing a glimpse of his beery face
as he drives off the bank of the Liffey.
With a grasp on the reins of his dray

he slants into flight immortal,
coat tails parting on the whole performance.
For an instant, his weight confounds the air
before he descends to a crapule of mud

and although I try to dodge his downfall
my great great grandsons will bear his brunt.

Nest

Move earth sip by sip
up to the eaves.
Secure walls
with articulated spit.
Dispense with foundations.
Believe. Bowl
eggs into place.
Avoid brooding.

Sit tight
incubate flight
sleep weather-wise.
Neb your chicks
then launch them.

Migrate. Return.

Journey

You always broke my fall
While I was running down
My love, my life, my all.
I ran into a Dane

While I was running down
The Finnish one who smoked.
I ran into a Dane
He liked the way I spoke.

The Finnish one who smoked
Was very good in bed,
He liked the way I spoke
About the Scot I said

Was very good in bed
(He's not as good as you).
About the Scot I said
It's time for him to go

(He's not as good as you).
I wanted you to stay
It's time for him to go
You held me straightaway.

I wanted you to stay
You always broke my fall
You held me straightaway.
My love, my life, my all.

Deer

Too often roadkill or sprung space,
our deer survive and come back north
pressing themselves to the house for warmth.
They're close enough to show their lice
teeming through fur that looks combed.
They'll bolden soon and scruff our fence
with moult, a herd of hoist-bellies
up for scraps they lick from my palms
on the day you venture out again,
all bristle and stink, warming to spring
with skin that's slackened on grief.
Gods from off the mountain, you'll say
in your grandiose way and stoop
while I kiss you in firm belief.

Horse's Mouth

To the people who claim this is not women's work,
I suspect Ruth would say *Think again*. Think again,
when she's eyeball to chin with a Blue Blagdon horse
who's allowed her to rasp a steel file on his teeth
without flinching. At first, you might waver and think

this appears medieval, especially the blood
which has bangled Ruth's arms, but you'll notice a hush
in the stable as well, an acoustic of trust
as she goes about freeing the horse from his *hooks*
of enamel, a job she calls *floating*. Unfazed

by the risk that those hooves could so easily rise
in the air and descend with a crash, Ruth persists.
If she didn't, that kick to her face years ago,
or the rivals who told her to quit would rear up
in her memory and bruise today's calm. At Bill Quay

she's unslept, having hiked overnight from the West
to raise money for kids, but her focus remains
on the Blue, which suggests the old proverb is right
when it says the way someone approaches a horse
is the way they approach the whole business of life.

Elizabeth Sheds her Inhibitions

I left them in a teal blue box
on a shelf above the lawnmower.
I locked the door on them quite firmly,
discarding the key down a well.

I then dug up the other keys
I had buried once out of fear.
Those were the keys I later left
in the lap of the homeless girl.

After snapping all the heads
from my husband's despicable roses,
I watered the weeds I love
and fed the crops to the cows.

I didn't eat, not a jot until dusk
when I served up four cold cuts.
I passed the port to the right and across
the space where the silver once sat.

By dark, I was riding bareback
on the horse I have seldom had time for.
Together we galloped all over the lines
laid down by neighbourhood dispute.

Lastly, I rode to see the young people
who queue in few clothes outside night clubs.
It was then I came across you officer.
And what a fine, fine officer you are.

The Life of Facts

1111

The midwife claps and counts
her blessings, fingers the caul
from the baby's head. She swipes
a cloth around the child to fish
for scraps of luck. She knows
the cloth will sell in strips
to seamen at the harbour
who'll wear it near their skin
to keep the world from running out.

1515

Holding my newborn in my hands,
I think of the wrong I've done.
My family will abandon me for dead,
when Upik tells them what he saw.
He's made *Inukshuk* of me, stitched
my hair in a bag of bones that vanished
through a sealhole. If I'm to live,
I'll need to go where sea ice bends,
where footprints melt around the brink.

2058

You want a boy so tick *Male*.
The doctor rigs pipettes
beside a window that's been rainy
now for months. You come to
Eyes, tick *Blue: no squint*. A tremor
rolls in from the coast, again
the building wavers. You check the pen
at *Feelings* where the column falls
away beyond the table's edge.

Waiting for the Wounded
– after the drawing by Muirhead Bone, 1918

Action has been suspended
and we become a drawing of breath
whilst waiting for the wounded

whose cries we hear exploded
a mile away in that bloodbath
where the rules have been suspended,

and though we'd run and tend them
we do not move; we clamp our teeth
instead, and wait for the wounded

soon to arrive, stumped, lopsided,
haemorrhaging gore, and faith
now the gods have been suspended –

we know such men can't be mended,
why our neat meal of tea and broth
will cool as we wait for the wounded,

that our wives will be astounded
when we refuse to doctor truth
about the wait, and the wounded,
how our lives have been suspended.

Fortune

You will wake up to snow outside
and drink, without chipping at ice.
You will eat meat you did not kill.

Even though you are a woman,
you will read a letter, twice.

You will speak the same language
as a girl you admire
and you'll do so without meeting.

You'll get rust in a cut
but it will not kill you.

You will make a child
with a man from abroad,
while looking at stars that have names.

You will stand
on a round earth that spins.

Your horizons will always be level.

Suggestions, please.

In the hospital corridors, bad art hangs
awkward as husbands who try to buck up
their dying. Stiff, by the snack machine,
a life-size dancer looms *en pointe*, contorts

her unscarred body. Opposite, the sea
on paper stretches out and stops, just short
of a size 10 bootprint stamped on the wall.
Yesterday, there was even a chicken

in Radiography, photographed twice –
first as an auburn bird in a field, next
as an x-ray version, gone queasy blue,
picking its way over nuclear heath –

before and after. Today, results,
and this waiting room with its vacant walls,
its sighing vents – an installation piece,
complete with miniature letterbox

labelled in bold, *Suggestions, please.* I think
I'd like a Rembrandt, for those who wait,
so someone will at last return our gaze
the Dutch-brown way a dog who loves us might,

or maybe, if we've space enough in here,
a print by that woman who daubed herself
in gold, then sprang at the canvas, saving
the one moment she managed to fly.

Armour

I'd rather be a lobster,
in pre-op, not knowing
whether I'll fail
on the surgeon's table.

The lobster has plans:

he can tear away
a limb in battle,
scrinch off home
and await new growth.

I've no such armour

only this ape's design
that frees my arms
to hold onto people
who'll shield my heart.

Madness, to a lobster

who keeps his head down
the shape of him claiming
that meat appears
that fight happens

miles from the ape

with her brain a fruit
in the treetops seeding
chatter and quips
while her fingers crack lice.

I wake up later

stitched into myself,
embracing the nurses
embracing you
making light

Three Dances

A Lesson in Quickstep for Strangers

In the aftermath
we've been learning to fly,
    this stranger I married
    and I. The secret, I find,
       is in short steps
       and following
while clearing the way.
I would dance
    twice as quick as time
    to free his heavy feet,
       to skirt dead ends
       and *keep it light.*

Our teacher's instructions
are for men's feet but mine
    do the opposite
    to make it work.
       With feathersteps,
       I try to lift
the weight of our difference.
I tiptoe. His hand flutters my back
    to make a new wing.
    He flaps
       at the edge
       of letting go.

Each window
is open tonight, *just in case*
    we pull it off, an airy dance
    for flat stones who trust
       each other
       enough

to balance and fly true
to skim the lagoon
        of a ballroom floor
      with a skip, skip

              and skip, skip and
              skip, skip, turn

Turn

Practice shoes fall to bits by the end,
fold in on themselves, stinkhorn-like.
Gold heels, built to wow, spend the night
bagged. Oxblood brogues trip the light
fantastique, then sulk in tissue, boxed.
Neat black pumps come to rest
in dressy-up chests and the
                   reason
                        is

this: that your feet want to go, cut a rug,
throw the floor out the door, and then
plant themselves tuber toes down in the loam.
They want to dib in to where dancing came
first, to a time when a foot could go gleaning
at night, to a time when your feet
would spin blood into children or wheat.

The Triple Mambo

Let's dance! he said
No chance, she said,
                        I'd rather
kiss, she said
like this and bopped
                        her fingers
down his spine,
then frisked his hairline
                        with her tongue
like this, she said,
like this. He said
                        he'd rather
stand apart
and watch her start
                        to want him,
watch her breasts buzz
through the fuzz of
                        That Black Top.
So watch me then,
she said, *you watch*,
                        her hips rolled
out of reach.
Just watch me pout
                        your name, she said,
her lips
jujubes for him
                        to eat.

I want your taste
he said, *come here,*

                  his short steps
stretched out long.
She touched his hand,
                It's time now,
Love, to do zig
zags, to do that
               cha
                   cha
               cha

One Who Adds

When you were born, we became similar,
your dad and I. We started to smile at
the same time because you were lovelier
than all the *good* boys. We never doubted
you'd be a different fruit, not when you ran
at dad in the blazing heat and called him
Bright-and-Orange. After that, you began
to say your dad and the sun were the same.
Or when you hopped towards me in the dark –
I turned you to the light and watched you shoot
across the yard in ecstasy. Suchlike
I'd not seen, least of all in a spacesuit.
I can hardly even remember us
from the days before you set us both loose.

Nit Nurse

Mention God and I think of the nit nurse
who sailed on a cloud of pink mohair
above the cheese polish floor of the Hall
where we herded to her, right from sermons
on love *Almighty*, to be in the fold
of her dough breasts, her tickle and talcum.

A part of me nuzzles there still, thrilled
by the way her fingers knew my earbones,
the way she tilted my head to the light
as if she were seeking a hallmark
before she would pause and register
the sum of my hairs, each one unharmed.

I sometimes wonder where she went,
if she basks in flamingo sunsets, abroad
while I hum and hah at the chemist's
over how to shrive my children's hair,
knowing she'd want me to home in
with a toothcomb rather than slick potions.

Compass

Instead of working, I put my arm round you
and we step back into the map of a journey
begun last week, onto shore, up rivers,
through forests of consonantal names
where gangs of illiterate mists crowd in
though you are undaunted, because you can read

these books where a boy and a dragon prevail,
where storylines shed their own skin and gleam,
where every opening page has a compass
set out in bold. And though we have argued tonight
we are reading now. We are entribed

on the baggy chair by the rickety lamp
in a pool of light which becomes a dot
along the line of your quest, from badlands
where some of our family still can't read,
to foothills where Paver, Funke and Paolini
point you towards the world's greatest mountains.

Hitchers

That was the summer of free lifts
over the limestone of County Clare,
scant miles at any one time in cars
filled with ducklings, cars that were rust,
cars made out of three cars
stuck together. Every journey bloomed
with talk about nuns, recycling bins,
hashish and scones, that drum
of bull semen riding along in the back.

We were newly-wed, and impossible
as the orchids which grew from rock
in that place, bright with disregard,
the way we go on flowering still
where so many said we would not.

Rush-a-tina

He's on her scooter, quick through the kitchen;
she has a twist in her tights and her temper;
he has no socks on; she's lost her bookbag –
toothpaste has spattered the walls –
she needs ten pounds for her dinner

but he needs eight pounds for those tickets;
she's scooting back from the kitchen –
tyre tracks have scribbled the hall floor –
he's put a mask on, now he's a werewolf;
she has no tights on; he's lost his mobile;

she's got his mobile but can't find the emu
that lives in her pocket; he needs a pound
for charity; she's scooting off to the kitchen –
someone has smashed all the pencil tips down –
he's made a web in the bathroom door

but she needs a wee; he's found a mayfly;
she needs a note to explain that we'll pay
for the damage; he's lost his best blue socks;
she's scooting back from the kitchen –
a major electrical fault has occurred

and none of the phones seem to work –
he gets her back up by taking her money;
she scoots across his big toe and his bookbag;
he's lost his plectrum but bellows the Beach Boys
at quadruple speed in a bash of strings;

she's in a twist; he's on a scoot
and no-one can find the right keys.

Portrait of a Marriage, with Chainsaw

We should have had a wedding cake
with this miniature scene on top,
where you're the tired Renaissance saint
and I'm a slasher movie Thing
beyond the fallen sycamore,
snarling a chainsaw at the gale.

You're right to say I never trained
for this, but I'm not listening now
I have these hailstones in my ears,
and don't want you to take the risk
away – I have my own ideas
on how to bring the garden back
and how to turn a grim machine
against what comes between us.

Ship

It's not just the war that bothers me,
or the fact that spring has gone missing,
it's more how the *Danio* ends up wrecked
on the same rocks as the *Forfarshire*
and for ten days we can see its arse,
that gash, the clumps of pubic weed,
how two thousand deadweight ton can sulk,
while the deck is rinsed of excuses
by six crew who simper to camera,
preferring not to admit their mistake
is one that's been made for centuries,
and their geo-plotting devices
won't save them from bluster, or lessen
the desperate need to pay attention.

How Mackie Did the Drowning, Plashetts

To begin, he moved into her kitchen,
slouched on a chair while she fried up *hinnies*.
He brought in pine cones, dubbin, swamped
her smell of cotton-scorch and Bibles.
Every night, to dry their tongues, he hung his boots
from bedrails near the stove. He slaked himself
on her, before he told her how he'd dammed
her river, how a flood would come. He stayed
a while, until the first wave reached the hearth,
until it climbed the panelling. He left
for higher ground, the day the waters floated
Jesus off the wall, back turned forever.

That's when he edged up Belling Hill, to watch
her rooftop disappear, her chimney brim with water.
The lake he made weighed four years.
Some days he thought he'd drink the lot
to fill the space inside him. Instead, he cast stones.

Plashetts – the drowned village beneath Kielder Reservoir, Northumberland

43

Footing

Before I became a wall, I was spread out as one big puzzle.
I was pulled from the burn and the field, and I was all in pieces.
I had always been there, before I was pulled, but not in this order.
Now that I stand between fields, I have ended an endless squabble.
Now I have bumpy shoulders, I am built to trip up the sheep.
I am built with strong sides, I am built out of forces, I balance.
Beneath my skin, I am full of patterns, I am full of hearting.
My footing is firm and it's broad: my footing is old as the fells.

Asylum Seeker

I came here in a coffin without handles.
Bruises healed. I began to dig gardens.
In Algiers, I was an archivist of bones.

Archival

Begin with the gaps

where the fibres show

each page is a tree, condensed.

With fingertips, read

the hand-made warp

of her times, the graze

where the parchment's been

neglected. Regret

the holes which reveal

your own skin back at you.

Rustle through leaves

that used to be boughs

of sap and birdsong –

touch between words

the breath

of what was a woman once.

Tradition

– Crowell's Boatyard, South Shields

It's what you make of it. Take it
or leave it a scatter of planks,
a leoparding wreck. Take it
you'll sweat yourself purple trying
to steam mahogany into ribs,
flare the frame like a giant's holding
of breath. Prepare to hop for miles
on feet that must be *budgie-like*.

If you're to clinch it, free from harm,
heel at the gaps with cotton caulk
before you deck it in flash
and gloss for the day you launch it –
back on the Tyne, *The George Elmy*,
your craft that weighs ten ton yet floats.

Trolleyology

I've given my life to these contraptions
so hope to answer all your questions
on why the Second Elizabethans
revered trolleys, enough to offer them
into the water that used to flow
along this valley you still call *Tyne*. I know,
as transport, they seem quite primitive –
let's not forget the people were limited
by their dependence upon the wheel –
and yet, as artefacts, trolleys reveal
the brightest glimpse we have of ancestors
who persistently failed to register
more than a scrap of their thoughts on paper.
When we read *Tesco*, or *Happy Shopper*
carved in plastic, we know the ancient tribes
were saying a trolley signified
where they belonged: it lent them a voice.
To give up a trolley meant sacrifice,
and yet the people were driven to it
for reasons we've now intuited –
it seems the Inter-Industrial Lull
shook people's faith in the Gateshead Angel,
driving them back to their northern River
where they attempted to gain its favour.
By giving it objects they most valued,
each tribe was asking the Tyne to renew
its bounty. Because we know what came next,
we must proceed with the utmost respect
ensuring our excavations focus
on trolleys, rather than all that bogus
Road Cone Theory or *Beercanology*,
for trolleys wield the most authority.

Harbour Master

You wear a shirt that's clean as light
and pilot this bank of machines,
to capture the Arctic storm in a graph
or summon Captain Sienkiewicz
on his slog through radio waves.
You throw him answers, marker buoy bright

but never look at the view or point
because you're in the business of knowing
everything out there's happened already:
in your mind's eye, that man
who's leaving the law courts now will jump
in the river, more likely than not;

the boatload of thugs and copper wire
will not be getting away with it;
at quarter past two, *Isolda* will sail
from Panama City, full of the fever
you'll keep at bay with a riddle
of experts and quarantine tape.

You try to bear with the present,
place a little red frame round the date
and nudge it along each morning,
cover your desk with fragile cups
to remind you of the rest of us:
the tourists in your high office

who'll never know how $N'8 = X$
or how to move a whole bridge,
or just how much those years at sea
could make you long for land, your children,
the reason you moor your moods in the neap
and always address the uncertain as *Sir*.

Meet the Victorians

Expecting a sermon, but finding an orgy
of sorts, I realise I've packed the wrong things,
and the shoehorn I brought, to extract myself
from the squeeze of uncalled-for gender roles,
seems out of place when Blondin's donkey is here
traversing a tightrope that's been slung up
between two chandeliers. My megaphone
for hectoring the women into voice
has been drowned out by the sound of the Queen
who laughs like a skunk, as Rosa Redquim,
Lord Crim-Con and Randiana begin
another round of Sub-Umbra, urging
Sport Among the She-Noodles. It's not quite
what I bargained for, having read Strachey
and come all this way to save Grace Darling
from patriarchal oppression. She's here
but not in person, perched at the lips
of the Aboriginal cricket team,
a transfer, rowing across their teacups
into the party, rowing decanters,
rowing glassware, rowing through gossip
and classic ennui, rowing collarbones,
rowing through Tabitha Tickletooth's soup –
an angel with oars for wings, unlikely
to fit beneath the lens I've lugged along,
or even stay put. There's far too much odd
stuff happening in corners and on the edge
of my vision, blurrings, a muffled scream
from inside the chimney, cholera sprigs
and servants who know how to read and write
by hoof-light. It's clear what I really need
are rollerblades, velocity, some chance
of gaining on Grace, or Victoria,

maybe making some sense of Darwin
who's whizzing along the hall with his kids
on a working-from-home piano stool.
If only I'd brought some juggling balls
or a dress made entirely of sherbert,
porn and fireworks, I might have captured
the party's attention long enough
to ask these men and women how they think.
Without such gear, I'm left to consult
the fat fob of my own time, wishing for
a thousand hands to help me grapple truth,
a cupboard where I might dump my luggage
and start to assemble the necessary
whale-sized bag full of open questions.

Grace Darling Learns to Count
– Brownsman Island, 1821

1 is a lighthouse, a person standing,
a finger raised, commanding *ssshhh* –
the course of a gannet's dive.

2 is a neb-nose duck out paddling,
a plane for wood or a girdling pan,
it's the cold squat of yesterday's iron.

3 is a guillemot tilting gales
4 is a sail in the Fairway tacking,
hoving a cargo of more numbers:

5 will hook on fast to memory,
8 will moor with a rope twist
round and around the docking horns

but 7 is harder, like the cut
in your sister's lip
only the Mainland mentions.

6 and 9 keep troubling you –
two whelks in a rock pool tumbling
away from any sense of up

but 10 is your mother at the spinning wheel;
it's you learning the world
whose numbers come to learn you.

Grace Darling's ABC

A

is the point of intention
she sees at the tip of her pen,
when guiding it over paper
to carve out her ABCs,

starting with A's composure,
its gable and its crossbeam
strong enough to house ideas
and hold a family of noises

various as the baby's *clack*,
her father's Sunday yawn
or, less pronounced, that bit of throat
she sounds before a song begins.

B

is the plump consolation
her father brings back from war,
when teaching her B is for *Bouche*
or *Bacioni* not just *bairn* –

a letter she fattens with ink
and practice, to bolster him
up from his memories. She writes it
as two kissy-lips beginning

to spell out 'Brownsman', her home
a roost of birds and books
where daughters can grow like sons,
embracing the broad horizons.

C

is the widemouth, hag-back, tongueless
retch of a letter on her lips
in the room where she dies, all *cough*
from her cobweb lungs, a threat

since childhood, when C would sigh
in the nest of her name yet croak
like a corvid without. Too hard
to prettify, as is what lies

beyond herself in her dying
on eider, when C marshals clot
and contortion, a life consumed
too soon, the slew of condolence.

D

is her mother's belly
pregnant with twins and drumming
against her palm – it's a dawning,
a full-blown declaration

on the Main, her mother's health
held high above the rumours
of why her father chose to marry
such an old wife. D stops loose tongues,

grows full of itself like the sail
on her parents' boat, their desire
to brood nine children out at sea
and pack each tight with defiance.

E

is the flight of three small steps
she climbs to reach the lantern room,
its wooden slats worn underfoot
and unremarked, a go-between

from dim hall to the drum of light
at the Longstone's head where she learns
her lessons – 'E for elevate',
'educate', The Enlightenment,

how the window panes are prisms;
that E refracts and warms all vowels;
why sunshine moves up rungs of print
in the long steep of her reading.

F

is the hole in a fiddle
where music opens, her father
playing a volley of Bach
at the sizzle and boom of storm –

fortissimo, how fun carries
notes louder than the Longstone's song
of threat, cold blood and shipwreck.
It's 'family' – how they press on

the way a bow persists at strings,
or breath can force past lip and teeth
to flourish out on a bare rock
as the fizz of human voices.

G

is her bitten-back tongue
gone soft on the sound of 'George',
a flavour of what lies hidden
behind Good Deeds and 'grit' and Grace

when her name is gonging the world –
G is gentler, the way he laughs
in the conch of her ear, his name
a nudge, through hundreds of letters

she'll burn one day to stop the Press
from gargoyling love after death,
and leave no trace in the hard-faced grate
but a grin of whitened ashes.

H

is the bond between people
she sees when her father shakes hands
with traders, or Thomasin grabs
at her wrist to keep her close, that hasp

in home and heart, here. She learns
how H is unspoken in honour
but stands its ground, a little bridge
for carrying breath into words,

fast as her grip on the stranded
the night of the Wreck, when she hauls
each numbed survivor over
from rock to boat and a safe berth.

I

is the seedling she grows
from a compost of guillemot shit
and stones, her tiny conductor
of life between air and soil,

outstretched as her way of saying *aye*
to every chance of garden
that holds its own against the salt
where she sprouts up through childhood,

finding I is how she writes
herself on the page as a stalk
with a knuckled root, a plumb back,
a bud at the head unfurling.

J

is a hook that hangs by a thread
in the vault of the North Sea
where it inkles, bright as her faith
the fish will come. Parabolic,

it's bent on 'Jesus', offering
bait like prayer to the cold blood
and gape of what she imagines
beyond the slack. J bides its time

when spoken, pent behind her teeth
before it bursts into voice as joy
at the landed catch and spatter
of cod, how answers arrive.

K

is the way she stands to shoot,
with her body a barb of limbs
and gun – a stiff salute to killing,
unshakeable as the need for food

but also the kick in kindness
that makes her send each bullet clean
through trailing birds only, her gift
of geese to Bewick and Hancock,

museums she'll never visit
where K is the unacknowledged,
her skill concealed within mute birds
like a shot that has no echo.

L

is the post and tether
her mother attaches her to
the day she learns to walk, love's tug
at her ankle, an island law

less rigid than it seems, L yields
lullabies, that place for lolling
inside her father's elbow,
the outer limits of her leash

where rockpools become her library
and she discovers her shadow
will send the shore crabs nimbling,
now she is both cause and effect.

M

is her *Macintosh* cape, draped
on the back of a chair to dry,
its vulcanised wings the drooping black
of cormorant or rumour,

Mainland malice, mutterings
about these gifts the Duke bestows,
the way she's 'mollycoddled', changed –
M hums its disapproval,

miles from the modern magic
of suddenly being sleet-proof
within her *Mac*, the warmest stretch
in a cold metamorphosis.

N

is a line on the weather chart,
plotting the course of winter
her first year, when summer truants
the whole country – a sharp nosedive

through black snow in June, it's squeezed
breath tamped inside her voicebox,
unresolved as hunger
when traders *nither* and bring *nowt* –

or need, how seagulls cram the lightbeam,
orbiting round the Lamp for sun,
her clamour in her mother's arms
for nurture, now, the nub of milk.

O

is that look of admiration
cast towards her fame's gold sun,
it's what makes her a hero,
the medal they pin to her front

quite something, yet also nothing,
O is the shape of a secret,
the coins she earns from salvage
locked in a drawer but haunting her,

all lined up as if to score
a requiem of silver Os,
flat as the faces of drowned men
she pulls from the sea like moons.

P

is her favourite puffin,
all beak, overreaching its feet
and perched as if about to tip
to italic, a paradox –

impossible as the Longstone Light
she sees being built on water
by engineers who conjure up
its flamboyant big-headedness,

cause for her *pfff* of scorn when told
about the need to move out there,
to turn her back on all her birds,
face east in the name of progress.

Q

is an egg with a pin stuck through
she holds in her palm, a quirk
in the ranks of the everyday –
it puffs itself out, insisting

she query, quiz and question
where life comes from, how it hollows,
whether an egg or bird came first
and where her petrel samples go

while she remains. Elliptical,
it's known as queer, the way she acts
round visitors, or needled says
'I would I'd been an egg and hatched'.

R

is a knot in the ribbon
she ties at her chin to secure
her best bonnet, as tight as thrill
along her throat, it announces

'Respectable' at Aidan's Fair
when tangling with Bamburgh dancers,
a Wheel of Fortune, and claggum
rictus. It's also release,

the way she loosens her tongue
with cousins whose R is a *burr*
that rolls the words until they growl
like dogs in a pack she belongs to.

S

is the swerving line of chalk
she draws across her slate to make
'snake', 'sun', the to and fro of 'sea'
revising stone – it's whispering

dust when she rubs it out, rewrites
its shape again, a meander,
the way she learns how letters shift
both in and out of sense, tell stories,

secrets slippery as sand eels,
her father's hush-hush smuggling
and salvage, wriggling away from church
when the sermon turns to saintliness.

T

is neater than how she feels,
when reading Thomasin's name
in winter, seeing the T as bold –
a mast above the storm.

Its square shoulders, its level best
are what she tries to emulate
when hurricanes coop her in
and bend the Longstone sideways.

Her letters fold their wings and wait
to flock to her sister in spring,
dreaming of mainland treetops
while perched at the tip of her tongue.

U

is the round-bottomed coble
she punts across the page to write
'our Universe', or keep 'us' afloat
above the line – a balancing,

unruffled as the way she holds
the oar and learns to row alone
her understanding of water –
it's how she skippers a new word,

five years ahead of her brothers
whose *oo's* freight the family crib,
fat with the chance of tipping up
but always rocking back true.

V

is the shape of migration
as geese go overhead in Spring,
or boats assert a cutwater
while bearing her sisters away

to mainland lives of children,
husbands, and hushed-up violence –
all she prays against, hands joined
when V is vehemence, and her vow

never to marry or compromise –
the wedge of hair between her legs
she touches till it transforms
her spread thighs into beating wings.

W

is a sudden wave
that swells inside her body,
gathering pace before it crests
as breasts that seem half skin, half sea

each time they fatten with the moon
or pool back in her armpits;
two points to be skimmed over
by tailoring and family talk

of 'woman', 'wife', 'due warning': words
that throw their arms up at her shape,
as halfway through her life she learns
her flesh now has an undertow.

X

is the multiplication
she uses to calculate beets
and births, how many birds she knows
by Latin names, the strangers saved,

each kiss she plants on George's shirts
when sewing, hidden treasure
marked by one stitch embracing
another – love's cryptograph

once fame sets in, her need to hide
behind a fence of crossings-out
on paper, how she practises
both autograph and expunction.

Y

is the tree with two branches
that stands in her sister's garden,
fruiting its own decision
to turn from the sea and eat sun,

but also the gannet mid-plunge,
choosing to dislocate its wings
day after day and continue
to turn from the sun and eat sea,

a divergence, the way she stands
arms raised, her body a 'why?'
each time her sister sails away
to the Main and leaves the family split.

Z

is a burst of Congolese
in the Bamburgh Castle library,
the day a *Zebra* springs at her
from page ninety-eight of Bewick –

a zigzag into the new
so rare, it dazzles her eyes
with its lightning bolt, auguring
times that will happen without her

when zoos will open and dizzy up,
the zoetrope spin her tale,
and words sprint on to catch the sense
of modernity's zip and zooming –